WEEKLY WR READER®
EARLY LEARNING LIBRARY

Great Americans
Andrew Jackson

Monica L. Rausch

Reading consultant: Susan Nations, M.Ed., author/literacy coach/
consultant in literacy development

Please visit our web site at: www.garethstevens.com
For a free color catalog describing Weekly Reader® Early Learning Library's list
of high-quality books, call 1-877-445-5824 (USA) or 1-800-387-3178 (Canada).
Weekly Reader® Early Learning Library's fax: (414) 336-0164.

Library of Congress Cataloging-in-Publication Data

Rausch, Monica.
    Andrew Jackson / by Monica L. Rausch.
      p. cm. — (Great Americans)
    Includes bibliographical references and index.
    ISBN-13: 978-0-8368-7683-3 (lib. bdg.)
    ISBN-13: 978-0-8368-7690-1 (softcover)
    1. Jackson, Andrew, 1767-1845—Juvenile literature.
  2. Presidents—United States—Biography—Juvenile literature.
  I. Title.
    E382.R265   2007
    973.5'6092—dc22
    [B]   2006032580

This edition first published in 2007 by
Weekly Reader® Early Learning Library
A Member of the WRC Media Family of Companies
330 West Olive Street, Suite 100
Milwaukee, WI 53212 USA

Managing editor: Valerie J. Weber
Art direction: Tammy West
Cover design and page layout: Charlie Dahl
Picture research: Sabrina Crewe
Production: Jessica Yanke and Robert Kraus

Picture credits: Cover, title page, pp. 5, 14, 17 Library of Congress; p. 6 © Gary W. Carter/CORBIS;
pp. 7, 8, 10, 12, 13, 19 © The Granger Collection, New York; p. 9 © North Wind Picture Archives;
pp. 15, 18 Charlie Dahl/© Weekly Reader Early Learning Library; p. 21 © Raymond Gehman/CORBIS

Printed in the United States of America

1 2 3 4 5 6 7 8 9 10 10 09 08 07 06

Table of Contents

Cover and title page: Andrew Jackson was the seventh president of the United States. His thick, red hair turned gray before he became president.

Chapter 1

The Hero of New Orleans

On the morning of January 8, 1815, about five thousand men waited and watched. From behind their long wall of mud, they saw the red coats of the British troops coming toward them. It was time to attack! The men of the United States army fought about ten thousand British soldiers. They listened to their leader, Andrew Jackson, and they won the Battle of New Orleans!

About two thousand British were killed or wounded, but the Americans lost only about thirty men at this battle. Andrew Jackson and his men were heroes. Jackson's skills as an army leader made him very famous. His skills and his fame helped him become the seventh president of the United States.

Winning the Battle of New Orleans made everyone in the United States very proud. The British had once ruled the United States. Now the people of the United States could show the British how strong they were.

"I WAS BORN IN S° CAROLINA, AS I
HAVE BEEN TOLD, AT THE
PLANTATION WHEREON JAMES
CRAWFORD LIVED ABOUT ONE
MILE FROM THE CAROLINA ROAD
X° OF THE WAXHAW CREEK"
ANDREW JACKSON TO J. H.
WITHERSPOON, AUGUST 11, 1824.

JACKSON SAID IN HIS LAST
WILL AND TESTAMENT THAT HE
WAS A NATIVE OF SOUTH CAROLINA

THIS STONE STANDS UPON
THE PLANTATION WHEREON
JAMES CRAWFORD LIVED,
NEAR THE SITE OF THE
DWELLING HOUSE, ACCORDING
TO THE MILLS MAP OF 1820.

Jackson was the first president born in a log cabin. He was born on March 15, 1767, near Waxhaw between North and South Carolina. His father died just a few weeks before Jackson's birth. He was killed in an accident while chopping down trees.

Two states claim to be the place where Jackson was born. This stone marks Jackson's birthplace in South Carolina, and another stone marks his birthplace in North Carolina.

Jackson, his mother, and his two older brothers lived with his aunt. When Jackson was thirteen, he and his brothers went to fight in the **American Revolution**. They wanted America to be free of its rulers in Great Britain. Jackson's older brother, Hugh, was killed. The British took Jackson and his brother Robert **prisoner**.

Jackson was only thirteen when he fought the British at the Battle of Hanging Rock in the American Revolution.

While Jackson was a prisoner, a British officer told Jackson to shine his boots. Jackson did not want to do it. The officer hit him with his sword, cutting Jackson on his hand and on his head. For the rest of his life, he would have scars there. He also would stay stubborn and strong willed.

Jackson did not want to obey the soldier. He was not afraid of the soldier's sword.

Later, Jackson's temper led him into other fights. Here, he is shown winning a **duel** with another man.

Soon after Jackson and Robert got out of prison, Robert grew sick and died. Then Jackson's mother became ill while she was nursing soldiers. She also died. At fourteen, Jackson became an **orphan**. He went to live with his relatives.

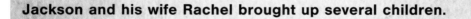
Jackson and his wife Rachel brought up several children.

When Jackson was seventeen years old, he began to study law. In 1788, he started working as a lawyer in Tennessee. At that time, Tennessee was part of North Carolina. Three years later, Jackson met and married Rachel Donelson Robards.

Chapter 2

A Military Leader

In 1796, Tennessee separated from North Carolina and became the sixteenth state in the nation. The people of Tennessee sent Jackson to Washington, D.C. He was their first U.S. **representative**. He then became their **senator**.

In 1804, Jackson bought this large farm in Tennessee and called it the Hermitage. He also owned slaves. They worked in the house and in the farm's fields.

Andrew Jackson soon came back home to work as a judge. Then, in 1802, he became the leader of Tennessee's army.

During a war between Great Britain and the United States, Jackson led this army in battles against some Indians called the Creek. (The Creek called themselves the Muscogee.) Some Creek fought on the United States' side, while others fought on the British side. In 1814, the Creeks lost the battles against the United States.

Jackson made the Creek sign a **treaty**. This agreement said all of the Creek — even the Creek who helped the United States win — had to give up their land. This land was larger than most states at that time!

The leader of the Red Stick Creeks met with Jackson to sign the treaty.

Because he was a strong and tough leader, Jackson's soldiers called him "Old Hickory." A hickory tree has tough, hard wood.

One year later, Jackson led U.S. soldiers in a fight against the British. At that time, the British and the Americans could not agree on where to put the border between Canada and the United States. The British navy was also attacking American ships and forcing Americans to work on British ships. In the Battle of New Orleans, Jackson's small group of soldiers beat a much bigger group of British soldiers. Jackson became known as an army leader and a U.S. hero.

In 1817 and 1818, Jackson fought the Seminole Indians in the land that is now Florida. He believed the Seminole were attacking farmers and helping escaped slaves hide. He also thought they were working with the British. Spain claimed this land, but it did not have a strong army in the area to defend it. In a treaty, Spain gave the land to the United States in 1819.

Jackson fought battles in many different places. Many battles were in the southern United States, including Louisiana and Florida.

Chapter 3

A Strong President

In 1824, Jackson ran for president. Many people voted for him, but the election results were unclear. The House of Representatives had to vote for one of the three leading men in the election. They voted for John Quincy Adams. In 1828, however, Jackson ran for president again and won.

John C. Calhoun was Jackson's first vice president. Unlike Jackson, he believed states could choose to not obey national laws.

Jackson believed that the president should be a strong leader. When he was president, Jackson **vetoed** many bills passed by Congress. He did not want these bills to become laws.

When South Carolina did not want to obey a national law, Jackson grew angry. He did not believe that states could choose which national laws they wanted to obey. He believed that all states should obey all national laws.

This map shows the Native Americans' homelands in orange. Their new lands in the West are shown in green.

Jackson also supported the Indian Removal Act. This act was a law that let the government make many treaties with the Native Americans in the eastern United States. The government forced many Native American groups to sign their treaties and give the United States their land. In return, the Native Americans were given much smaller pieces of land in the western United States.

While Jackson was president, more than forty-five thousand Native Americans were forced to leave their lands and move west. The United States took millions of acres of their land.

Many Native Americans died on their way west. The U.S. government did not give them enough food, clothing, or blankets for their trip. Many walked barefoot on icy roads.

Chapter 4

Going Home

Jackson was president for eight years. When his term was over, he went home to the Hermitage. He still had many talks with the next president, his friend Martin Van Buren.

Jackson died at the Hermitage on June 8, 1845. Today, people can visit the home of this strong, tough president and leader.

When Jackson died, the Hermitage was given to his son, and his son sold it to the state of Tennessee. The graves of Jackson and his wife are at the Hermitage.

Glossary

American Revolution — the war fought between the American colonies and Great Britain, which ruled them. In 1783, the colonies won and became free of British control.

claim — to state as fact or to say that something is owned

duel — a formal fight between two people with others who set the rules for the fight

national — describing or having to do with the whole nation or country

orphan — a child whose parents have died

prisoner — a person who is not free to move about and who is under the control of another person or people

representative — a person chosen by a group to make sure the government meets their needs and understands their concerns. A U.S. representative votes in the House of Representatives, one of two parts of Congress.

senator — one of two people chosen to represent a state in the Senate, one of two parts of Congress

slaves — people treated like property and forced to work without pay

supported — approved of

treaty — an agreement or a deal made between two groups

vetoed — refused to approve or to make something into a law

For More Information

Books

Andrew Jackson. American Lives: Presidents (series). Rick Burke (Heinemann)

Andrew Jackson. Photo-Illustrated Biographies (series). Steve Potts (Capstone Press)

Andrew Jackson. Presidents and Patriots of Our Country: History Makers Biography (series). Carol H. Behrman (Barnes and Noble Books)

Web Sites

American President Life Portraits: Andrew Jackson

www.americanpresidents.org/presidents/president.asp?President Number=7

Click on links to find interesting facts about Andrew Jackson.

Andrew Jackson

www.worldalmanacforkids.com/explore/presidents/jackson_andrew .html

Information on Andrew Jackson's life

Index

About the Author

Monica L. Rausch has a master's degree in creative writing from the University of Wisconsin-Milwaukee, where she is currently teaching composition, literature, and creative writing. She likes to write fiction, but sticking to the facts is fun, too. Monica lives in Milwaukee near her six nieces and nephews, to whom she loves to read books.